2, 4, 6
LEGS

Patricia Brennan

Rigby

I see two legs.
They are walking.

I see four legs.
They are resting.

I see six legs.
They are climbing.

I see eight legs.
They are working.

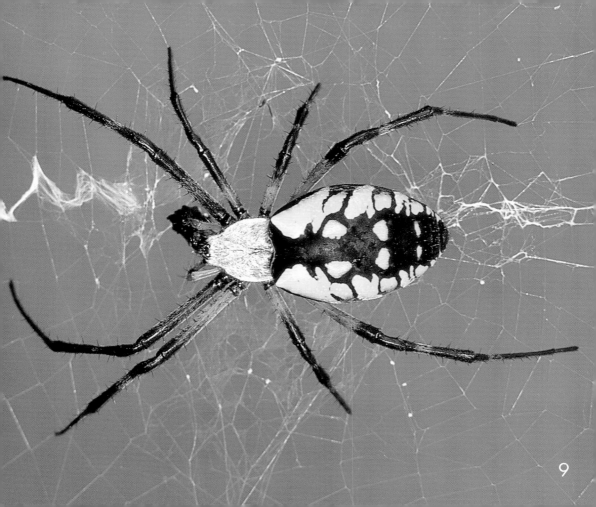

9

I see six legs.
They are jumping.

I see four legs.
They are running.

I see two legs.
They are skating.

Can you see legs?
I see no legs!